CAROLYN SNELLING

**CREATION
HOUSE**
A STRANG COMPANY

Ace by Carolyn Snelling
Published by Creation House
A Strang Company
600 Rinehart Road
Lake Mary, Florida 32746
www.strangbookgroup.com

Design Director: Bill Johnson
Cover design by Justin Evans
Author photo by Carrie Fay Amaro

Library of Congress Control Number: 2010920443
International Standard Book Number: 978-1-61638-153-0

First Edition

10 11 12 13 14 — 9 8 7 6 5 4 3 2 1
Printed in the United States of America

DEDICATION

*"If ye continue in my word, then are ye
my disciples indeed; And ye shall know the
truth, and the truth shall make you free."*

—John 8:31–32, KJV

The more we let God take us over, the more truly ourselves we become—because he made us. He invented all the different people that you and I were intended to be. It is when I turn to Christ, when I give up myself to His personality, that I first begin to have a real personality of my own.

—C. S. Lewis[1]

CONTENTS

ACKNOWLEDGMENTS

PASTOR PAULA WHITE AND HER AMAZING MINISTRY TEAM:

The fruit of the righteous is a tree of life; and he that winneth souls is wise.

—PROVERBS 11:30, KJV

THE MARY DANISON FAMILY:

The LORD shall preserve thee from all evil: he shall preserve thy soul. The LORD shall preserve thy going out and thy coming in from this time forth, and even for evermore.

—PSALM 121:7–8, KJV

THE MAN MENTIONED IN CHAPTER 1:

For it is commendable if a man bears up under the pain of unjust suffering because he is conscious of God.

—1 PETER 2:19

Mrs. Brown:

No man hath seen God at any time. If we love one another, God dwelleth in us, and his love is perfected in us.

—1 John 4:12, kjv

My amazing husband:

His mouth is sweetness itself; he is altogether lovely. This is my lover, this my friend.

—Song of Songs 5:16

Veterans and all who serve the United States of America:

I thank my God upon every remembrance of you.

—Philippians 1:3, kjv

INTRODUCTION

A GOLFER CANNOT POSSIBLY predict with any specificity at the beginning of a round of golf the score to be posted on his or her card by the end of the round. Many factors influence each round of golf and ultimately the golfer's score. Is the course familiar to the golfer? Are the day's weather conditions particularly blustery or sweltering hot? Is the golfer suffering with a bad back or bad mood that day? Maybe he or she is experimenting with a new swing technique. Regardless of these and other mitigating factors, no golfer has ever consistently achieved an under-par score for each round of golf played. It simply isn't possible.

What might be possible for the golfer, however, is to predict his or her response to each round, whether good or bad. Can a serious golfer find happiness in shooting a score of seventy-two when the day before the scorecard read seventy? Will a score of eighty or, heaven forbid, a ninety still bring joy to the golfer? In my case, I am elated if my card shows anything under one hundred, and that's just for nine holes!

An ace, or hole in one, is the lowest and best score a golfer can achieve on a par three hole. I have never had an ace, but I shouldn't really expect it, as I don't play much.

My husband Bob, a seasoned player, says there is no way a golfer can predict when or if an ace will be posted on a scorecard. In his sixty-plus years of playing, Bob fondly remembers all three of his aces. "Every golfer," Bob claims, "is always surprised when they score an ace; *however,* there is a swing a golfer can put on a ball that will raise anticipation and expectations of scoring an ace."

In my relationship with God, it has taken me a long time to realize just because I have accepted Christ as my Lord and Savior, it doesn't mean all my days are going to be aces! However, when I have a good day or one to be considered an "ace," shouldn't I predict with specificity how I will respond to God? Instinctively and intellectually, my answer should, of course, be yes. Singing His praises for a good day should be a no-brainer. But do I always offer Him praise when I should? Regrettably, I haven't. What about during bad or indifferent days? Can I also predict my response to Him? Regrettably, I can't.

If there is a particular golf swing that may lead to a "one" in golf, is there something we can do to raise our expectations of living a life one in Him through the good times and the bad?

It occurs to me if I have to ask this question, I am not living a life free in Christ. I am not living for the One.

> I am the LORD, your Holy One, Israel's Creator, your King.
>
> —ISAIAH 43:15

If you read my second book, *Eagle: Two Under Par and Soaring for God*, you may recall Bob asked, "What does it mean to be free in Him?" I smugly replied, "Honey, if you didn't get God's message of freedom in *Mulligan* and if it hasn't been made apparent to you now with *Eagle*, well, you will just have to wait for the third book, *Ace: One in Golf and One with God*." At that time I honestly thought I knew how to answer him, but God has provided the best response to Bob. In fact, my Savior's response was one I could have never imagined in my wildest dreams!

God began to reveal elements of His response in January 2009. He carried my learning through mid-November of that same year.

This story begins the evening of January 20, 2009. I was chasing our ever-jubilant and effervescent three-year old, eighteen-pound Poodle-Yorkie mix, aptly named Pookie, around the house. OK, now that you have stopped laughing at the thought of a middle-aged woman in hot pursuit of her beloved puppy, you can now envision me flying through the air and landing on my cold, unforgiving tile floor. Long story short, I ended up breaking the humerus—*not* so funny—bone in my right shoulder, my dominant side.

With my arm in a sling and physical therapy looming, I thanked God surgery wasn't needed, but now I was faced with a decision: carry forward with my online doctoral studies or finish *Eagle* while working through the pain?

I couldn't be at the keyboard eight to ten hours a day for school and write *Eagle* at the same time. The pain was too great, and a choice had to be made. I don't believe for one minute God caused the accident; it was totally my clumsiness. He knew it would happen, though, and as it turns out the accident was a blessing in disguise! If I had still been in school, I couldn't have finished *Eagle* when He knew I would. Furthermore, you would not be reading this book on freedom in Him right now if I hadn't fallen and been able to complete *Eagle*.

But if I am going to bring *Ace: One in Golf and One with God* into its proper opening perspective, let me fast-forward to September 2009.

It was a calm Arizona morning. The slightest hint of a cool desert breeze was in the air, which meant another season was about to turn. Fall was just around the corner. Similar to the profound question Bob had for me in *Eagle*, he had another question that morning relevant to this story and its beginning.

We were enjoying our one and one-half mile stroll with Pookie around the neighborhood. As we rounded the corner and headed for home, ever thankful not to have been attacked by a coyote (a concern for dog walkers in Arizona), Bob asked, "You know, honey, before we actually publish *Ace*, do you think you ought to get the help of a professional writer? Maybe a professional could help you express yourself in a way that might cause more people to hear what God is using you to say. You know what I mean?"

In all honesty, I knew exactly what he meant. Bob's heart is always concerned with making me happy. His intent was not to seek monetary gain, as that is never his agenda. His concern was for me to receive some affirmation other than a handful of sales confirming I was on the right track for God!

When God put it on my heart to write my first book, *Mulligan: A Second Chance at True Love and God's Grace*, my goal was never about being on the New York Times Best Seller list. In hindsight, maybe I should have prayed for that. Just kidding!

Mulligan is the story of God bringing me Bob, my incredible second husband. In golf, a mulligan is a golfer's opportunity for a do-over or a second chance. Our marriage has demonstrated in a most profound way God's unconditional love for me. I didn't and don't deserve God's grace, yet He offers it anyway.

The second book, as I mentioned earlier, is *Eagle: Two Under Par and Soaring for God*. In golf, an eagle means a golfer scored two under par on any hole. Being under par is a mark of excellence. God revealed to me in a two-week timeframe how we Christians can live an under-par life for Him.

With this third book, *Ace,* we will look at a celebration. In golf, an ace or a score of "one" will bring a golfer great joy. It has become clear, as I look back over my life, that in all aspects of our experiences, good or bad, we are meant to find celebration for and with Him.

These books in the G.O.L.F.: God Our Loving Father series are my way of celebrating the joy and freedom I have found in Him. My writing for God is an example of a portion of the C. S. Lewis quote in the front of this book, which says, "It is when I turn to Christ, when I give up myself to His personality, that I first begin to have a real personality of my own."[2]

My pastor, Lee McFarland, has been a huge help each week in his sermons, as he uses his in-depth Bible knowledge to help me express my joy. In fact, Pastor Lee is always encouraging the weekly attendees to dream bigger and happily display our gratitude for Him. Our joy in God might just help others understand so they, too, can know Him. I have thought about going to a Christian university to gain my own in-depth knowledge of the Bible and may pursue those studies at some point. But for now, thanks to Pastor Lee and other pastors I have met along the way, here's what I have learned:

- I know God created us and sent His Son to die on a cross to free us from our sins.
- I know Jesus offered us hope in trusting His Father.
- I know Jesus asked us to love one another.

- I know Jesus will return. Upon His return, He will take those of us who have accepted Him as the Son of God back to heaven with Him.
- I know if I write or don't write, He won't love me any more or less.
- I know I couldn't get through each day, good or bad, without Him.
- I know the only thing we Christians can do for Him is to somehow, some way tell or show others about the incredible and undeniable journeys He takes us on so we can all be free in Him.

So, I write.

Just as a golfer goes to the driving range to improve elements of his or her game, we who have said yes to Christ must be vigilant in praising God for taking us to the driving range of our lives. He wants to improve our game so we will ultimately understand freedom in Him.

In both *Mulligan* and *Eagle*, God gave me acrostics to make a point, and here is what He gave me for *ACE*:

A — A
C — Celebration of His
E — Everlasting freedom extended to everyone

In golf, an ace brings about a celebration for a few, but with God His celebration is for everyone.

When I write, there is a definite celebration taking place on my keyboard, much like the celebration that may ensue when a golfer scores an ace by giving a victory fist pump, a smile, or a leap.

I give a victory fist pump when God shows me a particular scripture for you that supports what I may be writing, like Galatians 5:1, "It is for freedom that Christ has set us free. Stand firm, then, and do not let yourselves be burdened again by a yoke of slavery." Yes!

I smile when He has me write something funny. I leap out of my chair when a book is finishing and He has given me an idea for the next.

It is for these reasons that I can't give my writing to a professional writer. Giving my writing to someone else to make it more saleable would make me feel as if I were sacrificing the relationship and freedom I feel in Him.

While C. S. Lewis expressed his feeling of freedom in Christ differently than you or I might, the point is the same: The more I feel Him in my life, the more I can use what He gave me to tell others about Him! Let's reread the Lewis quote, for I love the way he expresses himself.

> The more we let God take us over, the more truly ourselves we become—because he made us. He invented all the different people that

you and I were intended to be. It is when I turn to Christ, when I give up myself to His personality, that I first begin to have a real personality of my own.[3]

Perhaps you are thinking to yourself, *That sounds all well and good, Carolyn, but I don't like to write. So, how do I give up myself to His personality? I am not really sure I understand.* Or maybe you are wondering, *But Carolyn, how can I celebrate and praise God when my days seem filled with sorrow?* Or finally, *Carolyn, how can I know when I am truly free in Christ?*

If you struggle with these questions, please allow me to share how the One showed me how His freedom rings! God will provide you His answer to each question with its own chapter.

He shows me every day and in every way how I can put a swing on my life, as Bob says, to "raise anticipation and expectation" of living for:

A — A
C — Celebration of His
E — Everlasting freedom extended to everyone

If we have been united with him like this in his death, we will certainly also be united with him in his resurrection. For we know that our old self was crucified with him so that

the body of sin might be done away with, that
we should no longer be slaves to sin—because
anyone who has died has been freed from sin.

—ROMANS 6:5–7

Chapter 1

IN GOLF, CERTAIN CHOICES MAY LEAD TO VICTORY; *WITH GOD,* A CHOICE FOR HIM IS CERTAIN VICTORY

SHORTLY AFTER I broke my shoulder, Valentine's Day was upon us. February 14, 2009, will forever be significant as a day symbolizing love, most especially God's love. It was a day that began with tears of joy with the exchange of cards and ended with tears of sadness from the irreparable damage of a road rage bullet. But first, let's revisit some history and why Valentine's Day is still one of my favorites.

The origins of St. Valentine's Day seem steeped in speculation. Some historical accounts portray a third-century imprisoned saint with the name Valentine who fell in love with his jailer's daughter. He allegedly presented her with a card reading, "From your Valentine."* Other accounts claim the day was an attempt to make a pagan festival "Christian."

---

* See "History of Valentine's Day" at www.history.com/content/valentine.

Growing up in the late 1960s in northern California, I recall our parents offering me and my sister little gifts on Valentine's Day, usually something bearing a heart, maybe a pin or a necklace. The gift was always something that to us said, "I love you."

The first valentine I remember giving someone outside my family was in 1968. I was in the second grade at Olinda Elementary School. I was the "runt" in my class, complete with horn-rimmed glasses, a petite frame, and bobbed brunette hair.

Mrs. Rosalind Brown was my teacher. Her hands were soft and tender as she readily placed mine in hers whenever I was sad. She, too, wore horn-rimmed glasses; she was a kindred soul for certain. She had the brightest, happiest smile I had ever seen. She was one of the first in my life to teach me the value in caring for and loving another. I often think of her. She was African American, and racial tensions in our country were high at that time. I wonder now if those times were difficult for her or members of her family. If she experienced any strife, the only emotion she ever showed was pure love.

Mrs. Brown prepared our class for Valentine's Day by instructing us to make Valentine's Day card holders. She gave each of us one sheet of white and one sheet of red construction paper. We used Elmer's glue to paste heart-shaped white doilies onto the red paper. We then stapled the red paper onto the sides and bottom of the white paper, leaving the top open so the cards could be placed inside. If memory serves correctly, we used a handheld hole-punch to place holes on the top corners of the holder. We then wrote our names across its front.

We ran a piece of yarn through the holes, making a triangle-shape with the yarn and tied the yarn at its top so the holder would hang from pegs near the chalk-board at the front of the classroom. She instructed us to prepare a Valentine's Day card for each of our classmates and bring them to class on that special day. We even had to make cards for the boys—ew! Boys at that time in my life had what I affectionately referred to as "cooties."

My mom drove me to our local drugstore to buy cards for each classmate. As incredulous as it may sound to my younger readers, back in the day we didn't have card stores or malls to buy such things. C'mon now, you who are of my vintage; you know what I am talkin' about.

To top off the Valentine's Day celebration in our class, Mrs. Brown or one of our room mothers brought in home-made Valentine's Day-themed cookies and cupcakes.

I loved reading all those cards when I got home. Yes, even those from the boys. We partied pretty hard that day as I recall—well, as hard as second graders can party!

But in all seriousness, that Valentine's Day ranks highest in my memory because it was an innocent and simple expression of love, a single moment in time from our one true God, our one and only Valentine.

In my younger years, regrettably I didn't know God. Consequently, I made a lot of bad choices as I moved into my teens. But He knew me and was waiting patiently. What an incredible Valentine we have in God. He loved us first!

We love because He first loved us.

—1 John 4:19

&

Valentine's Day 2009 drew me closer to my one and only Valentine and marked a life forever changed. Bob and I started the day exchanging cards, kisses, and giving gratitude to God for allowing us one more day together. Bob always gets the best cards. We sit closely as we read out loud the card the other has given.

Bob has always celebrated Valentine's Day in an over-the-top way. On our first Valentine's together he took me to Disneyland for the day. Each year since has been something grand—an evening in concert with Johnny Mathis, to the theater to see *Phantom of the Opera*, an overnight stay in the mountains of Big Sur, California, etc.

I am certain Bob wouldn't have chosen those events for himself, except maybe the Johnny Mathis concert, but all the rest he did for me alone. He has always, always made an extra effort on this day to show me how much he cares. Yes, God has truly blessed me with an incredible husband!

There are some who say the day is a marketing scheme created by the greeting card companies. Others still ask, "Why do we need a single day to say, 'I love you'?" While there may be some truth to the statement and the question, if you are blessed to be on the receiving end of a Valentine's card or any gifts, you know the smile your heart feels. If you are on the giving end, you can also feel the joy you brought that special someone with your expression of love.

Our day continued with breakfast, reading Scripture, walking Pookie, and making phone calls to friends and family to wish them a joyous day. Bob arranged for a romantic dinner, complete with cracked and cleaned crab meat accompanied by fresh sourdough French bread sent to us overnight by one of our favorite San Francisco restaurants. My arm was still in a sling from "the Pookie incident," and we were looking forward to going to church on Saturday night and then returning home to enjoy this treat.

Before we could celebrate that evening, however, Bob and I heard about a man who had been shot while driving to work. Another car came along side his vehicle and shot at his car. He was seriously injured by a potentially fatal gunshot wound, but in spite of his condition, he was able to pull over to the side of the road and call 9-1-1. Yes, by the grace of God he was able to use the phone to call for help.

As Bob and I prayed for this man, I was struck by an important realization. While this day can be one of great joy for those of us who have someone to love, it can be very sorrowful for those whose loved ones have passed into our Lord's care or for those who suffer with illness.

It can also be a painful day when a spouse doesn't seem to think the day is important or to those who live in countries who don't know such freedom to enjoy the day. And you would suspect it to be an unbearable reminder to those who have been victims of senseless violence.

In all honesty, had I been in the place of the man who was shot on Valentine's Day, I would have undoubtedly been angry and cried, "Why, me?" On that day, however, kneeling before God when our pastor asked us to pray, I realized how very, very awesome and powerful our God is everyday and in every way. He cares for each of us uniquely, just as He did for this man by allowing him to call for help in the most dire of circumstances!

I realized that day He gave us the greatest Valentine of all—His Son, Jesus Christ. It is precisely because of His Son that we are able to show gratitude to God for every moment of our lives.

We can pray for others and help others. And, we can also thank Him for family, friends, and the people He sends as examples of His love in our lives—like Mrs.

Brown and Bob. We should thank Him in the good, bad, and sad times of our lives.

Each moment is cause for celebration. Why? Because our Creator has given us an unknown number of days here to celebrate His goodness, to show how He works in and through us, and to thank Him for all of it! We should greet each day, as Pastor Lee says, "before our feet hit the floor as we get out of bed" with a fist pump for Him, saying, "Yes!"

I have heard the man who was shot has deepened his relationship with God. Simply amazing.

༅

With any tragedy, the obvious question is, why does God allow such things to occur? I don't presume to know why God allows things to happen as they do. All I can offer is, perhaps He places before each of us circumstances in which we have the choice to willingly serve Him in whatever way we can, whatever those circumstances happen to be.

> So do not be ashamed to testify about our Lord, or ashamed of me his prisoner. But join with me in suffering for the gospel, by the power of God, who has saved us and called us to a holy life—not because of anything we have done but because of his own purpose and

grace. This grace was given us in Christ Jesus before the beginning of time.

—2 Timothy 1:8–9

He is our God and is without a doubt worthy of honor and praise, regardless our circumstances!

The Lord lives! Praise be to my Rock! Exalted be God my Savior!

—Psalm 18:46
A Psalm of David

Here is another God-inspired acrostic:

W — We
O — Owe our
R — Righteous God honor and
S — Show
H — Him
I — In
P — Praise

We should worship God for all He has done, most especially for sending His Son to die for each of us, removing our sin and offering us His grace. This is cause for the greatest celebration.

Although we Christians may do everything and then some to worship Him, we are never guaranteed a life that makes us feel like celebrating every single day. But if we say we trust Him, we must give Him our best, regardless of our circumstances.

Whether you are an incredibly caring and loving teacher like Mrs. Brown, who chose not to bring any personal issues to her job; or a generous and thoughtful spouse like Bob, who chooses to put aside his desires for his wife; or the man who was shot who chooses to deepen his resolve in Christ although he suffers physically, I offer my deepest thanks. You are all beacons of God's light in this world!

In good or bad times, shining and sharing His light regardless of our circumstances is why we are here!

- Are you celebrating the life our Valentine has given you?
- Are you worshiping Him for what He sends to you alone?
- Do you pray for others?
- Do you offer a simple, "Thank You," each morning?
- Do you sing to Him in church? Do you dance like King David did?
- How do you let your light shine for Him?
- Do you volunteer at your church?
- Do you help a neighbor in need?
- Do you still celebrate Him through the storms of your life?

Perhaps you're thinking, *But Carolyn, I am too sad to celebrate. I am physically sick. I am hurting emotionally, too. I am going through a divorce. I have no hope. I have days when I can't stop crying.*

I, too, have been where you are and wouldn't dare attempt to offer these thoughts if God hadn't brought me through.

Remember, you are not the first to experience sorrow. Jesus knew sorrow, too—a sorrow deeper than anything we will ever experience. He totally understands. In John 11:33–35 we read this account from after the death of Lazarus:

> When Jesus saw her weeping, and the Jews who had come along with her also weeping, he was deeply moved in spirit and troubled. "Where have you laid him?" he asked. "Come and see, Lord," they replied. Jesus wept.

We read this from when Jesus was in the Garden of Gethsemane:

> He took Peter and the two sons of Zebedee along with him, and he began to be sorrowful and troubled. Then he said to them, "My soul is overwhelmed with sorrow to the point of death. Stay here and keep watch with me."
>
> —Matthew 26:37–38

Matthew 27:46 describes the scene at Jesus' death:

> About the ninth hour Jesus cried out in a loud
> voice, "Eloi, Eloi, lama sabachthani?"—which
> means, "My God, my God, why have you
> forsaken me?"

Despite His sorrow, Jesus dedicated His life to
remaining perfectly consistent with regard to His Father,
the Scriptures, and the reason He was sent. He was one
with God in everything He did, even though He knew
great sorrow. Why? For you and for me!

Let's not for one second allow Christ's death to be in
vain! He died so we would have a choice to say yes to a
life with Him and His Father. Regrettably, there are some
who proclaim, "No, I will figure things out on my own."
Some others claim, "No, I can't believe in a God who
would allow such bad things into my life. And then you
want me to praise Him? No thanks. He is not for me."

Perhaps you are in one or both of the "no" groups. Or
maybe you know someone who is in those groups. At one
time that was my choice, too. It would be my privilege
if you would allow me in the following pages to show
how three golf concepts might show you the benefits of
making a "yes" choice of knowing freedom in God.

Those concepts are:

- keeping things simple,

- course management, and
- staying hopeful

If you have decided to read on, thank you!

Chapter 2 begins in a place I had never been. It is a place of great honor and cause for celebration in America. It is the site of a great battle. It stands today as a last bastion of fighting for freedom at any cost.

It is the Alamo.

> You, my brothers, were called to be free.
>   —GALATIANS 5:13

Chapter 2

IN GOLF, THE SIMPLE IS COMPLEX; WITH GOD, THE COMPLEX IS SIMPLE

THE INFAMOUS BATTLE at the Alamo in 1836 has become legendary for the show of heroism on the part of a couple hundred Texans. These brave men valiantly attempted to defend their position against General Santa Anna and his scores of soldiers.[4] But the event, however, is not remembered in the defeat but rather in the stance for freedom.

Ironically, when God took Bob and me to San Antonio, Texas, home of the Alamo, in May 2009, He gave me a simple understanding of what Christ did by dying for all of us. His death at Calvary was His stance for everyone's freedom. It is just that simple.

He died so each of us could leave sin behind, be one with Him, and enjoy a freeing relationship in Him. But if you fight the idea of freedom in Him by choosing not to be a freedom fighter for Him, how can you anticipate all the wonderful things, places, or even people God sends you?

Why, oh why, do we make our relationship with Him so complex?

Similarly, there are those of us who manage to complicate the game of golf, too. Many golfers struggle with the game and make it more complex than it should be. My hubby has a more simplistic approach to the game, and it's called practice. He and many others like him will achieve lower scores more readily by diligently practicing both on the driving range and the putting green. His chance of success is far greater than those of us who are more like Rene Russo's character in the golf movie *Tin Cup*.

Russo's character arrived for her lesson with the golf professional, played by Kevin Costner, looking like the quintessential new player. She had the appropriate attire, complete with a golf watch, the latest clubs, and golf training gadgetry. With her training gadgetry piled on her body at once, she looked ridiculous. Costner's character gave her a good scolding for being an embarrassment to the game. *He threw aside those things that were holding her back from improving her game.*

In golf, the simple can get very complex, very quickly and very easily. Not only are there the trappings of the training tools, but the number of thoughts running through a golfer's head can be mind-numbing. "Keep my head down. Don't swing too fast or too slow. Be sure to shift my weight. Rotate my shoulders properly.

Focus on the ball. Stay behind the ball." Ugh. It can be overwhelming.

When all these thoughts permeate the golfer's mind at once, the results are usually not what the player anticipates. Yet, we all do it, except for the professionals, as they seem to have trained their "swing thoughts" to be simple. They know the importance of the K.I.S.S. principle. You know, the Keep It Simple, Silly principle. Some of you may have heard the word *stupid* substituted for the word *silly*, but I thought *silly* sounded better.

While the game of golf can get complex, God has made a life celebrating Him very simple.

But Carolyn, God is way too complex! He made the heavens, the earth, oceans, all the creatures, man, woman—and that was only in the beginning! Look at how He has allowed us to develop in terms of medicine, technology, space exploration, etc.

I fully understand and give all credit, glory, and honor to our Creator. He understands far more than we do or ever will.

> Great is our Lord and mighty in power; his understanding has no limit.
>
> —Psalm 147:5

He is perfect. He is God. He is everything. I know! What I am suggesting is, for all His wonder, might, and glory; He wants to be our Friend, our Savior. He wants to keep it just that simple.

He could have made it more complex, but He didn't. You may recall in the Old Testament it was the Israelites who managed to complicate things, not God. God was very clear and simple in His expression of who He was and what He wanted for them. He kept it just that simple.

> I will take you as my own people, and I will be your God. Then you will know that I am the LORD your God, who brought you out from under the yoke of the Egyptians. And I will bring you to the land I swore with uplifted hand to give to Abraham, to Isaac and to Jacob. I will give it to you as a possession. I am the LORD.
>
> —EXODUS 6:7–8

ೋ

Shortly after Valentine's Day, my mind raced toward *Mulligan*'s debut in May. I wanted to tell as many who would listen what God had done by sending me Bob. Our family and close friends knew our love story, but I wanted to broaden that audience.

I have to pause here and ask you a question. Are you like me, thinking you must help God? If you said yes, thank you! Now I know I am in good company and not alone in my Type A, have-to-always-be-in-control behavior.

In my effort to help God, I spent a fair amount of my small inheritance from my parents to advertise *Mulligan*. The predominance of the advertising was through Strang's in-house advertising magazines and email blasts.

Once that was done, I thought the wise thing left to do was pray. I know my priority was out of whack; prayer should always be first.

So, I prayed, *Dear Father, if You want Mulligan to touch lives I leave it to You.* It was a simple and heartfelt prayer. There was no way I could have imagined in my wildest dreams how He was about to answer.

The month of March was upon us before we could blink, and Bob and I were preparing to receive out of town guests. March in Arizona is generally quite lovely. It is a time when we Arizonans try not to think too much about the looming heat of summer. Instead, many of us eagerly anticipate the "boys of summer" bringing back our national pastime, baseball. In *Mulligan*, I mentioned that baseball is one of my and Bob's favorite sports. Our families and friends enjoy the game, too, and use that time of year to visit, especially since a spring training ballpark is a few minutes from our home. I can already smell the hot dogs and fresh peanuts wafting through my memory bank!

As with any time we have company, I managed to complicate their arrival. I always seem to clean parts of our home they will never see. I buy way too much food, which we are left with long after the guests are gone. In addition, that particular March, I had to send *Eagle* to the publisher before they arrived. Needless to say, it was very busy, and I was still only functioning with one arm.

During all this chaos, the last thing I expected was my wonderful Counselor and Friend to answer my simple prayer. Yet, that is precisely what He did. He is always there for us. It is just that simple.

It was March 18, 2009, a blessed day for certain! My best girlfriend of over twenty years, Georgena Rickey, and her husband, Randy, had left our home earlier that morning after a three-day visit. During their visit we took them to a baseball game, Georgena and I shopped 'til we dropped, and she and I treated ourselves to pedicures. It was an awesome time, as we can always just be ourselves with our great friends. While we did our "girl" thing, Randy and Bob played golf and visited a large golf store in northwest Phoenix—their "guy" thing. (I know, I know, girls play golf and shop in golf stores too!)

Anyway, after Randy and Georgena left for home, I was feverishly trying to get sheets and floors washed and our guest bedroom and bathroom cleaned, as Bob's daughter, Teri; our son-in-law, Terry; and our two grandsons, Cameron and Austin, were to arrive in a couple of hours. Crazy timing, I realize, but it worked the best for our guests!

With most of the cleaning finished, thanks to the help of my hubby, and the sheets in the dryer, we decided to grab a quick bite to eat on our patio. It was a crisp, sunny day, and the golfers were lined up on the men's tees located adjacent to our backyard. We thought we would spend a few minutes watching them tee off.

I brought my phone out to the patio, as we were waiting to hear that Teri and the rest of the family had arrived and were on their way. Just after hearing that they were going to eat lunch and then rent a minivan so we could all travel together anywhere we went, I received an e-mail—a short message from my publisher.

> Carolyn:
>
> Paula White is interested in having you on her program. Below are some possible dates:
>
> April 1–2, 2009
>
> May 6–8, 2009
>
> The taping would be in San Antonio. Please let us know ASAP. May might be the best since it is after the release date.

My immediate thought was, *Um…what?*

I couldn't believe my eyes and began to choke on my turkey sandwich. I am not quite sure if it was the choking or the sudden widening of my brown eyes that caught Bob's attention. He said, "What's wrong?"

After I swallowed my bite of half-chewed sandwich, I read him the e-mail. He said, "This must be a joke. Tell Strang it is a little early for an April fool's joke."

For the first time in my life, I didn't know what to say, so I wrote back to my publisher and asked for more details.

Here was my publisher's response:

> She is very well known internationally and in the Christian and non-Christian markets. She pursued us for the interview. Her TV show is syndicated on a lot of Christian stations and some non-Christian stations. She was the cofounder of Without Walls International church in Tampa, Florida. This is a huge interview to land.

Again, *Um...what?* My head was in a fog!

I told Bob what my publisher had said, and he just kept saying, "I can't believe it."

I texted Pastor Lee, and he said, "Wow, she is like the Christian Oprah!"

I called Georgena and another girlfriend of mine from

church, Natalie Hearn, and their response was, "What are you going to wear?"

As soon as Teri and the family walked into the house, Bob was in the most talkative state I have seen in our sixteen years of marriage. He visited Pastor Paula's Web site and proceeded to tell the family what had happened.

But wait. During all of this I forgot to stop and thank God. I was too wrapped up in the complexity of the moment. It wasn't until before I went to bed that night, while I was saying my prayers, that I thanked Him. I then remembered my simple prayer from the month before: *Dear Father, if You want Mulligan to touch lives, I leave it to You.*

And then it hit me. I had not done one thing to pursue an interview with Pastor Paula. God had orchestrated this interview, not me. It was for His glory that *Mulligan* would touch lives. There is no way possible I could have, as a first-time author, gained such favor from an international pastor, had He not supernaturally intervened. Praise Him forever!

I found myself asking, "Why me, God? I don't want to embarrass You. I am not worthy to represent You."

> But Moses said to the LORD, "If the Israelites will not listen to me, why would Pharaoh listen to me, since I speak with faltering lips?"
> —EXODUS 6:12

Then I remembered something Pastor Lee tells the Radiant Church attendees all the time. "God," he says, "doesn't always call the qualified, but he qualifies the call."

> You are to say everything I command you, and your brother Aaron is to tell Pharaoh to let the Israelites go out of his country.
>
> —EXODUS 7:2

Lying in bed, I began to cry. I was overwhelmed. I prayed again. *Dear Father, please keep me calm and represent You as You want.*

Well, of course He will do that! I know, I know, but sometimes I feel like I don't know what to say or how to pray, most especially in a moment like this, one I had never experienced before, in which He completely blew me away! Aside from simply thanking Him, I didn't know what to say.

The rest of the time with our family came and went. We went to a couple of ball games, a movie, and stayed up late playing board games. As my youngest grandson, Austin, was about to get into the car when they were leaving, he paused, ran back to where I was standing, and gave me a hug. In that moment, I honestly forgot all about a television interview. In that moment my grandson's hug, a perfect "ace," was reason enough to simply thank God!

For the benefit of those of you who might be saying, "Good for you, Carolyn. You are now a successful author. But I am still suffering. Nothing like that has happened to me. How do you expect me to celebrate God?"

Well, it may help you to know the following.

Pastor Paula's television show, where God took us on May 5, 2009, aired on August 14, 2009. As I chronicle these events for you, I do not have a clue as to the extent of the lives He touched with *Mulligan.*

In any case, God may have specifically used me to speak to one person in the studio audience that day. Maybe a marriage was on the brink, and He used my example to show how important marriage is to Him and to provide that person with hope. So, my success is in the knowledge that God answered my prayer in His way.

I don't know if you can relate to what I am about to say next, but it fits me to a "tee."

Too often, I treat God as if He were a genie in a bottle. I want Him to grant me the wishes I want for myself. I manage to complicate my relationship with Him by saying, "Oh, if only You do this, then I will do this." Who am I to treat our Creator in that manner?

But when I prayed those two simple prayers, God simply responded.

I prayed, Dear Father, if You want Mulligan to touch lives, I leave it to You.

His response: He took me to the *Paula Today* show,

and He will touch lives. I may not ever know the extent of His reach, but that is of His choosing.

I prayed, Dear Father, please keep me calm and represent You as You want.

His response: When Bob and I were in the green room, the area where guests wait before they are escorted into the studio, we read Scripture, and I prayed once again for calm. During the entire trip and throughout the interview God kept me supernaturally calm.

Of course, when I started to talk too much during the interview, I started coughing and couldn't catch my breath, but that was me getting in the way! Praise Him for the blessing of editing! God put the answers in my mouth to Pastor Paula's questions, and before I knew it, the experience was over.

You might have thought as soon as we arrived home from San Antonio, I would have gone straight to my keyboard to write all this down. But I didn't. I knew I would never forget the events. And in all honesty, for some reason I had been procrastinating in writing this portion of the book.

Do you suppose it is a coincidence I am now finally writing about the concept of freedom in Him on this day, Veteran's Day, a day in America when we remember those who have sacrificed so much for our freedom? On this day especially, I thank God for our veterans, but I also want to thank Him for sending me to the keyboard to express gratitude to His Son, who gave His life so I might know freedom in Him. He is simply amazing! (If you haven't read *Eagle*, I encourage you to do so, as His coincidences there are mind-boggling. Clearly what we call coincidences are simple reminders from Him of His presence.)

Speaking of coincidences, the day we arrived in San Antonio we went to the River Walk Mall and, of course, to the Alamo. We ate dinner at a Mexican restaurant on the River Walk. The day was Cinco de Mayo, Mexico's Independence Day—just another coincidence, perhaps. We took a boat ride around the River Walk. The boats were named for people in the area. Our boat was named *Miss Caroline.* I kid you not. Probably just another coincidence? Ha!

In all seriousness, it is entirely possible I may never know the reason He took us to San Antonio. It was a surreal experience and one I will always treasure. Pastor Paula White, her staff, and volunteers were extremely gracious hosts. They are mighty warriors for God, and to be with them, even for a short period of time, was as if I was in a dream.

From the moment we arrived to the time we left, we were greeted with a "Yes, Ma'am" and "Yes, Sir." The Southern Christian hospitality shown to us was like nothing I experienced before or since. I will be forever grateful to God for allowing us such an experience. It is almost too much to put into words.

> Sing to the LORD a new song; sing to the LORD, all the earth. Sing to the LORD, praise his name; proclaim his salvation day after day. Declare His glory among the nations, his marvelous deeds among all peoples.
>
> —PSALM 96:1–3

In chapter 1 when I spoke of tragedy, I realize what God had me write there holds true during the celebratory times too:

> With any tragedy, the obvious question is, why does God allow such things to occur? I don't presume to know why God allows things to happen as they do. All I can offer is, perhaps He places before each of us circumstances in which we have the choice to willingly serve Him in whatever way we can, whatever those circumstances happen to be.

As I close this chapter, what, then, can be said for simplifying our relationship with God? How can we begin to put that swing on to raise our expectation of an *ace*, a celebration of His everlasting freedom extended to everyone?

Well, if we examine Bob's success in golf through his hours of practice and the professional players with their simple and few swing thoughts, we, as Christians, may want do likewise in our relationship with God.

Doesn't it make sense to practice what He has asked us? However, before we practice, we will probably want to understand the fundamentals by learning what He has said through His Word. Simply read the Bible.

> But these are written that you may believe that Jesus is the Christ, the Son of God, and that by believing you may have life in his name.
>
> —JOHN 20:31

Doesn't it also make sense to keep your minds clear of the nonsense satan tries to send our way? Think simply on the wonderful things of this life.

> Finally, brothers, whatever is true, whatever is noble, whatever is right, whatever is pure, whatever is lovely, whatever is admirable—if anything is excellent or praiseworthy—think about such things. Whatever you have learned or received or heard from me, or seen in me— put it into practice. And the God of peace will be with you.
>
> —PHILIPPIANS 4:8–9

In the Introduction one of the questions and subsequent statements I thought you might consider regarding freedom in Him was, "How do I give up myself to his personality? I am not really sure I understand."

Well, the simplest thing you can do to give yourself to Him is to acknowledge your similarity to the Rene Russo character from *Tin Cup*. Tell Him, "God, my life feels burdened and weighed down."

The next thing you can do is to ask Him to be your "golf pro." Tell Him, "God, I want to learn the fundamentals of who You are and what You want for my life, so I pray for You to help me *throw aside those things that keep me from a freeing relationship with You and Your Son.*"

Yes, it is just that simple.

> Rid yourselves of all the offenses you have committed, and get a new heart and a new spirit. Why will you die, O house of Israel? For I take no pleasure in the death of anyone, declares the Sovereign LORD. Repent and live!
>
> —EZEKIEL 18:31–32

Here's another quick thought:

J — Jubilant for
O — Our God
Y — Yes!

Go on, give Him a smile, a happy fist pump, or a little jump for joy. He is waiting!

Chapter 3

IN GOLF, WE MANAGE THE COURSE; WITH GOD, HE MANAGES OUR COURSE

TILL REELING AFTER our trip to San Antonio, we felt like celebrating! Aside from worshiping Him that weekend in church, we honestly felt like jumping for joy, screaming at the top of our lungs, and generally acting like a couple of kids. OK, I admit I was feeling much more childlike than Bob. He is not much for jumping and screaming, but he was genuinely thankful to God for the incredible experience.

So as conservative adults—most of the time—where could we go that would be a socially acceptable outlet for such behavior? Well, it was mid-May, almost time for some schools to break for the summer, and we thought, What better time than to visit Disneyland, America's happy land!

Disneyland, located in Anaheim, California, is a short, six-hour drive away from our home in Arizona. It only took us about a tank of gas to make the trip. We reserved a very inexpensive hotel room. I hoped it didn't have cockroaches, as it was so inexpensive. We got AAA-discounted park tickets, and off we went. If you are anything like us, repeat guests to Disney, you probably have a plan when you enter the park to eat at your favorite restaurants and ride all your favorite rides at least twice. You may even plan out the rides based on the ones for which you know you will need to get a FASTPASS!

As soon as the park opened we headed straight for this awesome restaurant on Main Street. We ordered scrambled eggs cooked to perfection and crisp bacon, complete with home-style potatoes and grilled onions, which were totally scrumptious. We topped it all off with a mug of piping hot cocoa and a dollop of whipped cream.

After we ate, we headed straight for the rides that wouldn't jostle our stomachs too much, thus potentially ruining our delicious meal.

If you have visited Disney or any other theme park you may have noticed the different people and the items they carried. Some carry or wheel in the strollers huge diaper or tote bags for their young family. Most teenage girls carry little, tiny purses just big enough for their cell phones. Then there are some women sporting "fanny" packs buckled snugly around the waist. Yup, if you've seen that you were probably looking at me.

My pack is strategically stuffed with a cell phone, lip gloss, driver's license, medical card, hand sanitizer, Band

Aids, toothpicks, and a Bayer aspirin. The aspirin is in case one of us has a heart attack, the other can administer an aspirin. OK, stop laughing! The older I get, the more items I carry to meet any of our medical needs; it is just a fact of life. Bob carries the money, and off we go ready to conquer the park.

At the end of our first day, having had a wonderful experience, we went back to the non-cockroach–infested hotel. As we unwound from the excitement of the day, I jotted down some notes for this book. It occurred to me that my park preparations are strikingly similar to the methodology used by professional golfers as they go about their "play." Their preparations, however, are referred to as "course management."

Professional golfers and the better amateurs calculate how they will play each shot. They know which clubs will provide them with a specific yardage. Dependent upon previous experience with a particular hole and their current score, they may play a hole conservatively or more aggressively. Invariably, they do their best to avoid sand traps, water hazards, and out-of-bounds areas. Staying in the fairway gives the golfer the best opportunity for success. *Sometimes, however, the golfer isn't always able to manage the course as he or she had planned.*

On the second morning, before we left to conquer Disney: Day 2, we read Scripture and were getting showered and dressed when we turned on the television. We were watching a sports channel and learned about a professional golfer whose wife and mother had simultaneously been stricken with breast cancer. I instantly prayed for the family and then realized that despite our plans and preparations—our attempts at managing the course of our lives—sorrow does not elude any one of us.

> Be merciful to me, O LORD, for I am in distress; my eyes grow weak with sorrow, my soul and my body with grief. My life is consumed by anguish and my years by groaning; my strength fails because of my affliction, and my bones grow weak.
>
> —PSALM 31:9–10
> A PSALM OF DAVID

We returned home from Disney thankful for a safe trip and that God kept us healthy, ever praising Him that neither of us needed a Bayer aspirin!

After we had been home a few days, we decided to see the Disney movie *Up*, an adorable, family-friendly flick. Once we got home from the movie, Bob said he was feeling a bit "down." You must understand, for my never-complaining husband this was quite a declaration. By the grace of God, it appears as if he had a twenty-four hour flu bug and nothing more serious than chills, fever, and body aches.

The next morning, however, he was supposed to play in a golf tournament, one he had already pre-paid and in which his friend was relying on him to play. Substitute players cannot be readily identified in these situations. So, my selfless husband woke up and choked down his breakfast, but I could tell there was absolutely no way he was back to normal. Bob has degenerative arthritis throughout his body, most particularly in his back and spine, due to a car accident, and he really doesn't know what it would feel like any longer to be "normal." I am crying as I write this, as a drunk driver has left Bob in constant pain ever since he was nineteen. However, he still goes on with a smile and thanks God. Clearly, though, that day he wasn't back to his version of normal.

I told him not to worry about the money he had pre-paid to play in the tournament. "It's not worth your health," I said.

"I can't let my friend down," he responded.

He and his teammate went on to win their division in the tournament that day. Bob told me later he prayed to God, "Please just get me around today, not for me, but for my friend."

That moment in time was cause for celebration for Bob because God helped him play through the pain, plus gave him and his teammate a victory!

A few mornings after he and his friend won their division in that tournament, he was going out to play again, and I knew he was tired. Playing golf twice weekly is about all his body can now endure. Once again, looking for the easy way out—as I tend to do—I said, "Why don't you stay home, honey? It's not important that you play today."

He offered this very profound reminder. "Every time you tee it up is important, honey."

Well, that about sums it up, doesn't it? Each day of our lives, God gives us the opportunity to "tee it up" for Him. Will we, like Bob, play through the pain of our days and find a way to honor Him? Or will we, when we end up in our own hazards, feel defeated and not find the courage to still worship Him and thank Him for the day and the current situation?

Please believe me when I say I wouldn't ask you to do anything I don't expect of myself.

At this point many of you may be thinking, *She certainly doesn't understand the depths of my sorrow.* To be sure, I don't presume to be able to fully comprehend the depths of anything that may bring you sorrow. But perhaps a bit more insight into my life will give you greater pause to realize I may be able to empathize more than you know.

In my life, I have experienced physical abuse. Yes, I have had broken ribs and a split lip, and I have even endured being locked in a room, night after night. Although I fought sleep, as I never knew when my captor would arrive, morning always came, and my captor would greet me by dousing a bucket of cold water on me.

This was the best of that time.

After I finally escaped, I was greeted at my safe haven with, "What did you do?"

The accuser, a.k.a., satan continually attempts to haunt me by reminding me of life-altering choices from my past.

I have sat alone, several times, while Bob was in surgery, praying the doctor wouldn't say, "I'm sorry there is nothing more we can do. He's gone."

I have rubbed the feet of my dear girlfriend as she lay dying, while at the same time giving her morphine to keep her comfortable.

I read from the Book of Colossians to my mother as she lay dying, wondering how much she heard or took on her heart. I read Psalm 23 at her deathbed, and again at the deathbed of my mother-in-law.

When my father passed, I was only twenty-one and didn't know Jesus. As I laid next to him as he was dying, I felt helpless and cold.

My doctor continues to provide me quarterly checkups to determine if, indeed, I am in the early stages of leukemia. Praise Him; all is still well.

> I lift up my eyes to the hills—where does my help come from? My help comes from the LORD, the Maker of heaven and earth.
>
> —Psalm 121:1–2

But it is time to turn from my sorrow, as all Christians at some point must do. Let's turn to two examples of sorrow far greater than anything you and I will undoubtedly ever experience, unless of course you are a veteran; then perhaps this story is all too familiar for you.

It was the Fourth of July when I wrote this; perhaps just another coincidence. As most Americans realize, this is a day for great celebration. It is a celebration of the men and women who endured unbelievable suffering so you and I would be able to enjoy our many freedoms. I often take for granted each July Fourth, looking on it as a day to enjoy a hot dog and some homemade potato salad. The seedless watermelon was especially sweet and sticky on my fingers this year. I decided to buy pound cake and top it off with whipped cream for dessert. I suppose I should have opted for the apple pie, but I didn't. Bob and I watched baseball on television and then sat out on our back patio to enjoy the fireworks that lit up the sky from our local stadium. While the brightly colored fireworks burst in the sky, I felt a single tear trickle down my cheek as I thought about a television show I had watched the night before.

On July 3, I tuned into Christian television. A program recorded several years earlier, just after 9/11, was airing. At the time, we were just about to send troops to Iraq. On the program, there were a couple of veterans of the Vietnam and Korean Wars talking about their experiences.

I sat on the couch crying like a baby as I watched it. I couldn't believe the stories these men were telling, and with such calm demeanors. They were extremely articulate and lucid in their explanations of the horrific events in their lives as they fought for our country. The first gentleman was a retired air force general. He was in solitary confinement for four years! Unexplainably, the enemy let him out one day to join the others. The first thing he and his brothers did was hold an impromptu church service. There was a choir of four, a chaplain, and forty-two others. Many of them had not spoken in such a long time, yet they managed after reciting the Pledge of Allegiance to find a way to sing to our Lord. They were told after they had quickly met that they were not to worship again or they would be severely tortured. Well, by a unanimous vote of all forty-seven they decided to risk torture and worship again.

The other veteran who spoke was explaining the enemy's version of torture, which was a world apart from our interrogation methods. As the enemy attempted to "influence" this veteran into being a traitor to our country, he held firm in his faith. He was tied to a chair and forced to keep his eyes open for three days and nights while watching colored lights moving in a swirling direction with words on it. They wanted him to learn the words as evidence of his betrayal. How did the soldier respond? Well, in his mind he starting reciting Scripture from his youth, a youth spent in North Carolina under the tutelage of his grandfather, who was a pastor.

As if that torture wasn't enough, at the end of the three days, the enemy then hog-tied him. The ropes were tied in such a way around his neck that if he struggled he would have strangled himself. When they then threw this man in prison after a period of time, he prayed God would take him. He then said there was such a light in the jail after he prayed that prayer that he knew God was with him.

With continued horror I sat listening to this man as he told the last gruesome detail that time would allow. The enemy was marching the prisoners to who-knows-where when the veteran was able to escape by falling down a very steep mountain. He was shot at and left for dead, but our vet did not move. One by one other prisoners attempted the same escape, and their bodies kept piling atop his. From the bottom of the pile, he whispered to them all not to move. Soon he realized that none of them was moving any longer, the breath leaving each. Before long, there was no movement but his. He struggled to free himself from the mound of corpses, and he silently made his way to cover. In the cover of darkness he prayed to God, "Dear God, I don't know where I am. I don't know what to do. Please help me." He then heard God answer back, "Son, when have I ever left you?"

As I sat in the comfort of my living room, I felt overwhelmed. I felt so incredibly thankful to God for all He has done to richly bless my life. I never had to endure such suffering; in fact, quite to the contrary my life has been one big Fourth of July picnic!

I then sat in utter amazement at the fact of how there have been so many men and women, as those on this program and, of course, my father during World War II, who have suffered beyond anything you or I can possibly imagine. They risk their lives so you and I might know freedom.

Remember with me if you will, the apostles Paul and Peter, beaten and imprisoned. And most especially, what of our Savior, who was beaten with a lead-tipped whip, pierced on a cross, and stabbed—for what?

For you and for me.

On that Fourth of July when we hung our American flag in front of our house, I saluted it. I am so proud to be an American. The freedoms we enjoy are unequalled. We are the greatest country in the history of our world. It hardly seems enough, but I will continue my prayers for our men and women in uniform around the world, for our veterans who have fought so hard for us. There are many who died or whose lives were forever changed for me. Please, please join me in my prayers for these amazing people, and next Fourth of July take a moment to remember as you attend your picnics and barbeques what an unknown someone did for you.

In fact, why not take your lives and use them to give thanks to the "known" someone, Jesus Christ, who died so we might all know eternal freedom, so you might know an *ace*, a celebration of His eternal freedom extended to everyone.

Are you are able to celebrate God, as these veterans did?

In the most desperate and dire circumstances of your life, can you continue to praise Him?

Coincidentally—ha—Bob and I were reading the Book of Job when I wrote this. If ever there was an Old Testament example for us to learn from about suffering, it was Job. Clearly, Job suffered mightily, and yes, God allowed satan to test him.

> The LORD said to Satan, "Very well, then, everything he has is in your hands, but on the man himself do not lay a finger."
>
> —JOB 1:12

After satan laid waste to Job's livestock, killed farmhands, and killed his children, Job still worshiped God.

> Naked I came from my mother's womb, and naked I will depart. The LORD gave and the

LORD has taken away; may the name of the
LORD be praised.

—JOB 1:21

Apparently, satan wanted to bring an end to Job's
praise for God. He replied to God in Job 2:4–6:

"Skin for skin!" Satan replied. "A man will give
all he has for his own life. But stretch out your
hand and strike his flesh and bones, and he
will surely curse you to your face." The LORD
said to Satan, "Very well, then, he is in your
hands; but you must spare his life."

So despite being covered in boils, Job's clarity of
thought in his reply to his wife's rebuke of God shows
us a beautiful example of how we can affirm God on His
terms.

He replied, "You are talking like a foolish
woman. Shall we accept good from God, and
not trouble?" In all this, Job did not sin in
what he said.

—JOB 2:10

As Job's troubles increased:

- Did he curse the day he was born? Yes.

- Did he feel as if he had the right to complain? Yes.
- Did he feel helpless before God? Yes.
- Did he feel as if God hated him? Yes.
- Did he argue with God? Yes.
- Did he ultimately repent of his pity-party? Yes.
- Did God bless Job in the second half of his life even more than in the beginning? Yes.

For me, Job is a perfect example of what it means to feel freedom in God. Job acknowledged God's love in his life as He blessed him abundantly. Job aligned himself with Him by attempting to live by His ways. Then when Job was tested, despite his multitude of complaints, he continued to affirm, or stand firm, in God.

After God spoke to him, Job recognized his ignorance in questioning God's wisdom:

> Then Job replied to the LORD: "I know that you can do all things; no plan of yours can be thwarted. You asked, 'Who is this that obscures my counsel without knowledge?' Surely I spoke of things I did not understand, things too wonderful for me to know. "You said, 'Listen now, and I will speak; I will question you, and you shall answer me.' My ears had heard of you but now my eyes have seen

you. Therefore I despise myself and repent in dust and ashes."

—Job 42:1–6

Job, like others before him, including Moses and Aaron, Noah and David, actually spoke to the Lord. And the Lord spoke directly to them.

In all my boo-hooing, I would have probably gotten a grip if God spoke directly to me too, but God has never spoken to me the way He did to Job. Read Job 40 and 41 and you will see what I mean. God tells him of a behemoth and a leviathan, scary creatures to be sure, ones I don't think I ever want to see! Yikes!

So how can we affirm, stand firm, or express dedication to Him when we haven't had the benefit of speaking to Him directly? How do we rise up from our pity parties and praise Him when we choose to believe He is not there?

I love the Casting Crowns song "Praise You in This Storm." I think it provides us a great answer in our quest to rise above, which we must do if we are to find freedom in Him. I always listen to this song on my iPod when I am flying, as it helps keep me calm. It is one of my very favorite contemporary Christian songs.

Here are the lyrics:

I was sure by now, God, that You would have
 reached down
and wiped our tears away,
stepped in and saved the day.
But once again, I say amen,
and it's still raining.
As the thunder rolls
I barely hear You whisper through the rain,
"I'm with you."
And as Your mercy falls
I raise my hands and praise
the God who gives and takes away.

And I'll praise you in this storm,
and I will lift my hands,
for You are who You are,
no matter where I am.
And every tear I've cried
You hold in your hand.
You never left my side.
And though my heart is torn,
I will praise You in this storm

I remember when I stumbled in the wind,
You heard my cry to You
and raised me up again.
My strength is almost gone.
How can I carry on
if I can't find You?

And as the thunder rolls
I barely hear You whisper through the rain,
"I'm with you."
And as Your mercy falls
I raise my hands and praise
the God who gives and takes away.

I lift my eyes unto the hills.
Where does my help come from?
My help comes from the Lord, the maker of heaven
    and earth.
I lift my eyes unto the hills.
Where does my help come from?
My help comes from the Lord, the maker of heaven
    and earth.*

Before we head to the next chapter, let me share a story about an impeccable woman of great faith. Her name was Mary, and she was the mother of a very, very dear friend of mine, Debbie.

The psalm I quoted earlier, Psalm 121, was Mary's favorite. It's probably just coincidental that the Casting

Crowns song "Praise You in This Storm" is based on this psalm.

I had not known Mary long, only about a month, before she passed into our Lord's care. It was just long enough for me to realize how dear and important our Savior was in her life.

Debbie was headed back to Pennsylvania in late June to early July to welcome her new grandson into the world. She was reluctant to leave Mary, knowing she seemed to be in her last days. However, Mary was getting superb care and wanted Debbie to go. In Debbie's absence, I went to the care home and read to Mary from her beloved prayer book. Debbie joked, "Mom would even read to us from the prayer book when she drove us kids in the car."

One day before I was to read to Mary from her prayer book, I asked her, "How are you feeling today, Mary?" By now she was very frail, not taking in food, but agreed to the sip of water I offered. She said with a smile, "Oh, fine. I could always be worse."

I wish I could have taken a picture of Mary's bright smile as I held my cell phone to her ear so she could hear Debbie's voice on the other end telling her the good news of the birth of her tenth great-grandson, Isaac!

I feel amazingly blessed that these past eleven months God has allowed me to encounter so many wonderful examples of His children who praised Him through the sorrows and the storms of their lives:

- The man from chapter 1 and his devotion to Christ.
- Pastor Paula undoubtedly has her own personal struggles, yet she gives her all each day to advance God's kingdom.
- Sweet Mary knew every minute of every day how God had her covered.
- Bob never complains but is grateful for each day God has given him.
- Our veterans' perspective on suffering is beyond anything we will likely endure, and yet they still turn to God through it all.

I salute all of you. I cannot believe the blessing God has bestowed on me by bringing you all into my perspective. Never, ever will I forget any of you and who you have been for Christ.

My friend Debbie and I were with sweet Mary as she breathed her last breath. What a privilege God allowed me in reading Psalm 121 to her one last time while she was here on Earth.

It was July 10, 2009, at 1:50 p.m. that Jesus said, "Welcome home, Mary. Well done, my good and faithful servant." Even though Mary's passing was a time of great sorrow, she knew exactly where she was going and whom she was about to meet. For this reason, it was also a time of great joy, as we who knew her feel blessed beyond words for that reunion.

꒳

Despite our attempts at the course management of our lives, we must realize we will know sorrow.

I hope Job's story, along with the veterans' stories, have adequately answered the second question from the Introduction, How can I celebrate and praise God when my days seem filled with sorrow? These people whose stories I have told praised Him, and look what they went through. We can do it, too!

I also hope Mary's words of encouragement—"I could always be worse"—will help you throughout your days.

Coincidentally, on the day I finalized this chapter and was writing about Mary, I received a card from one of her sons, Paul. He wrote, "I think my mom would have been pleased by her service. It was a memorial of her life, but most of all it honored God." What an awesome Christian family!

By the way, my incredibly sweet and gentle husband offered up this reminder for Debbie as he offered his condolences: "Just remember, Debbie, your mom is in the best place she can be, Happy Land!" He must be hoping to head back to Disney!

By the way, Disney was holding a parade while we were there, and it was called, Celebrating Today. To me, someone writing a book about celebrating Him, it was another obvious coincidence. Let's celebrate each day, not for ourselves, but for Him!

Sorrow is better than laughter: for by the sadness of the countenance the heart is made better.

—ECCLESIASTES 7:3, KJV

Godly sorrow brings repentance that leads to salvation and leaves no regret, but worldly sorrow brings death.

—2 CORINTHIANS 7:10

Quick thought:

S — Sharing
O — Our
R — Realities Can
R — Ripen
O — Or
W — Wound

Wouldn't you want to be known as "ripen-er" and not a "wound-er"?

Chapter 4

IN GOLF, OUR HOPE IS IN OUR RETURN TO THE COURSE; *WITH GOD*, OUR HOPE, OF COURSE, IS IN HIS RETURN

WHETHER A PROFESSIONAL, an amateur golfer, or simply a weekend hack like me, a good score on a particular hole makes for fond memories. I play so rarely and so poorly—a result of rare play—it is pretty easy to remember when I score well. If you read *Eagle*, you may recall my enthusiasm for scoring a net eagle on the seventeenth hole of the Kona Country Club in 2008. When, by the grace of God, we returned in 2009, I was convinced if I scored well before, surely I could shoot that score again. Unfortunately, I ended up with a seven on that hole, *yet I still played on with hope.*

The game of golf is just that way. As I said in the Introduction, "There are no guarantees of a particular score on a particular hole," yet we who enjoy the game remain hopeful each time we play each hole. I believe God hardwired each of us to be full of hope. I think, however, He also hardwired us to make our own choices regarding whether or not we hope, or whether or not we love or know freedom in Him. The choice is clearly ours.

In the closing chapter I will explore some final thoughts on choosing Him or not, but for now let me take you back to May 28, 2009, a day when God expressed His explanation of hope in Him in a most profound and perfect way, by using His Word. Brace yourself, this next story should give you chills!

Bob and I didn't read Scripture first thing that morning, as we normally do each and every morning. On that day, a neighbor was bringing her dog over at ten o'clock in the morning so we could "babysit." Her husband was going into the hospital for outpatient surgery, and she didn't want to leave her baby home alone. (That surgery was successful, praise God!)

Additionally, we had been asked to take some morning pictures around our golf course for the promotional video we were having made for *Mulligan*. We had to get the pictures done early, as the golfers would soon be on the course and we needed to get back home by ten o'clock for our neighbor.

We got everything done and arrived home around 9:15 a.m. Instead of reading Scripture, I felt an overwhelming sense that God was encouraging me to write. Bob reminded me we hadn't yet read the Word, and I told him I thought it best to read after our neighbor's dog arrived and had a chance to settle in with Pookie; Bob agreed. I went into my home office and wrote the following:

As we near the end of the book, I can only imagine that some of you must be thinking, *Great, Carolyn, we are happy you have found a lot to celebrate about, but I will never know such things. I can't really relate.*

Well, perhaps you won't have the same happy experiences I have, but surely you can identify times when you knew God created moments that were just for you, such as a graduation, a wedding, a new baby, a successful surgery outcome, or hearing the words, "You are in remission."

Some of you, to be sure, have suffered in different and more extreme ways than I. Perhaps you have lost a child or children to death, which has brought on unimaginable suffering. Perhaps you or your child has been unexplainably ill for years or you are widowed or you have been in a life-altering accident. I want you to know my heart and prayers are forever with you. In no way do I mean to diminish your sorrow. However, I do know there is hope, and His name is Jesus Christ.

Each one of us has been given the freedom by God to choose His Son, regardless or especially because of our circumstances. Once we accept Him, it seems important for us to choose to move through, as best we can, all things that come our way. With great joy there will be great sorrow.

Life may not seem fair or just to us now, but He holds each one of our tears.

He said in John 16:33, "I have told you these things, so that in me you may have peace. In this world you will have trouble. But take heart! I have overcome the world."

It is becoming increasingly clear to me that we cannot possibly know great joy if we don't understand great sorrow. We cannot understand what is good and true if we haven't seen that which is bad and false.

The tree of this life bears a fruit called "choice." Sometimes things happen for which we have no explanation; other times things occur to which there is a very clear explanation. It is our response to the circumstances we find ourselves that, I believe, interests Him. Certainly, He understands our sorrow.

Jesus wept at the death of Lazarus. He gave us the ability to cry. He knows we will have a period of mourning in our lives. I don't know what that period should be, for it is different for everyone. But I do know that when we think we can't go on, He gives us an alternative.

When we are sad, not only will He bring people to cheer us, but He will also put people in our path, knowing they need cheering too. Can we move beyond our sorrow to encourage someone else? Will we continue to be sad? How will we respond?

Regarding when we feel angry or frustrated, He knew there would be times in our lives when we would be upset with Him and our life circumstances. But He never said we wouldn't be without trouble in this world just because we have accepted Him in our lives. But, He does offer us the church as a means of learning more about Him and the reason He died for each of us. Will we continue to be angry or frustrated? How will we respond?

If you are feeling lonely or depressed, remember He knows how long each of us will be on this earth. He also knows the number of hairs on our heads. That is how much He cares. You are never alone! If you have no family members left, is it possible to connect with friends in Christ or a church family? How will we respond?

When we feel we are without hope, we must take heart in Romans 5:3–5: "…But we also rejoice in our sufferings, because we know that suffering produces perseverance; perseverance, character; and character, hope. And hope does not disappoint us, because God has poured out his love into our hearts by the Holy Spirit, whom he has given us."

When we finally respond by saying yes to God's way, we will know freedom in Him. He is hope:

H — He
O — Offers
P — People
E — Everything

Once you know hope in your heart, then you can and you will celebrate!

After I finished writing the above, it was about 10:45 a.m. The dogs had worn themselves out after a fifteen-minute romp around the house, and we all settled in to hear God's Word.

In *Eagle*, I wrote about times when God offered some incredible, in my face reminders that it was His story.

Well, there I was again, listening to His Word offering me clarity that *Ace: One in Golf and One with God,* too, would be His story.

The Bible Bob and I read from each day is *The One Year Bible, New Living Translation.* Each day has a passage or passages from the Old Testament, New Testament, a psalm, and a proverb.

Each Scripture passage on May 28 related back to what I had just written between 9:15 a.m. and 10:45 a.m. As it was Bob's turn to read, I couldn't believe what I was hearing.

In order for you to truly appreciate what I experienced I have reprinted the passages from that day's devotion here.

> Now David's son Absalom had a beautiful sister
> named Tamar. And Amnon, her half brother,
> fell desperately in love with her. Amnon became
> so obsessed with Tamar that he became ill. She
> was a virgin, and Amnon thought he could
> never have her. But Amnon had a very crafty
> friend—his cousin Jonadab. He was the son of
> David's brother Shimea. One day Jonadab said
> to Amnon, "What's the trouble? Why should
> the son of a king look so dejected morning
> after morning?" So Amnon told him, "I am in
> love with Tamar, my brother Absalom's sister."
> "Well," Jonadab said, "I'll tell you what to do.
> Go back to bed and pretend you are ill. When

your father comes to see you, ask him to let Tamar come and prepare some food for you. Tell him you'll feel better if she prepares it as you watch and feeds you with her own hands." So Amnon lay down and pretended to be sick. And when the king came to see him, Amnon asked him, "Please let my sister Tamar come and cook my favorite dish as I watch. Then I can eat it from her own hands." So David agreed and sent Tamar to Amnon's house to prepare some food for him. When Tamar arrived at Amnon's house, she went to the place where he was lying down so he could watch her mix some dough. Then she baked his favorite dish for him. But when she set the serving tray before him, he refused to eat. "Everyone get out of here," Amnon told his servants. So they all left. Then he said to Tamar, "Now bring the food into my bedroom and feed it to me here." So Tamar took his favorite dish to him. But as she was feeding him, he grabbed her and demanded, "Come to bed with me, my darling sister." "No, my brother!" she cried. "Don't be foolish! Don't do this to me! Such wicked things aren't done in Israel. Where could I go in my shame? And you would be called one of the greatest fools in Israel. Please, just speak to the king about it, and he will let you marry me." But Amnon wouldn't listen to her, and since he was stronger than she was, he raped her. Then suddenly Amnon's love turned to hate, and he hated her even more than he had loved her. "Get out of here!" he snarled at her. "No, no!" Tamar cried. "Sending me away now is worse than what you've already done to me." But Amnon wouldn't listen to her. He shouted for his servant and demanded, "Throw this woman out, and lock the door behind her!" So the servant put her out and locked the door behind her. She was wearing a long, beautiful robe, as was the custom in those days for the king's virgin daughters. But now Tamar tore her robe and put ashes on her head. And then, with her face in her hands, she went away crying. Her brother Absalom saw her and asked, "Is it true that Amnon has been with you? Well, my sister, keep quiet for now, since he's your brother. Don't you worry about it." So Tamar lived as a desolate woman in her brother Absalom's house. When King David heard what had happened, he was very angry. And though Absalom never spoke to Amnon about this, he hated Amnon deeply because of what he had done to his sister. Two years later, when Absalom's sheep were being sheared at Baal-hazor near Ephraim, Absalom invited all the king's sons to come to a feast. He went to the king and said, "My sheep-shearers are now at work. Would the king and his servants please come to celebrate the occasion with me?" The king replied, "No, my son. If we all came, we would be too much of a burden on you." Absalom pressed him, but the king would not come, though he gave Absalom his blessing. "Well, then," Absalom said, "if you can't come, how about sending my brother Amnon with us?" "Why Amnon?" the king asked. But Absalom kept on pressing the king until he finally agreed to let all his sons attend, including Amnon. So Absalom prepared a feast fit for a king. Absalom told his men, "Wait until Amnon gets drunk; then at my signal, kill him! Don't be afraid. I'm the one who has given the command. Take courage and do it!" So at Absalom's signal they murdered Amnon. Then the other sons of the king jumped on their mules and fled. As they were on the way back to Jerusalem, this report reached David: "Absalom has killed all the king's sons; not one is left alive!" The king got up, tore his robe, and threw himself on the ground. His advisers also tore their clothes in horror and sorrow. But just then Jonadab, the

son of David's brother Shimea, arrived and said,
"No, don't believe that all the king's sons have
been killed! It was only Amnon! Absalom has
been plotting this ever since Amnon raped his
sister Tamar. No, my lord the king, your sons
aren't all dead! It was only Amnon." Mean-
while Absalom escaped. Then the watchman on
the Jerusalem wall saw a great crowd coming
toward the city from the west. He ran to tell
the king, "I see a crowd of people coming from
the Horonaim road along the side of the hill."
"Look!" Jonadab told the king. "There they are
now! The king's sons are coming, just as I said."
They soon arrived, weeping and sobbing, and
the king and all his servants wept bitterly with
them. And David mourned many days for his
son Amnon. Absalom fled to his grandfather,
Talmai son of Ammihud, the king of Geshur.
He stayed there in Geshur for three years. And
King David, now reconciled to Amnon's death,
longed to be reunited with his son Absalom.

— 2 SAMUEL 13:1–39, NLT

This story demonstrates on every level what I wrote
just an hour before I heard this scripture.

First, when I wrote, "Some of you to be sure have
suffered in different and even more profound ways.
Perhaps you have lost a child or children to death," how

could I have known I was just about to hear of King David's son being killed at the hands of another son? What an unbearable pain!

Second, I wrote, "Life may not seem fair or just." How could I have known I was just about to hear of Tamar's plight? Through no fault of her own, she was raped—and by her brother, no less! Indescribable sadness!

Third, I wrote, "The tree of this life bears a fruit called "choice." Sometimes things happen for which we have no explanation; other times things occur to which there is a very clear explanation. It is our response to the circumstances we find ourselves that, I believe, interests Him." How could I have known about Absalom's choice to actively plot and then carry out the murder of his brother? What an undeniable sadness and burden, one he most certainly carried his entire life. Although, Absalom was a pretty bad guy, what with later overthrowing his father David. His life ended shortly thereafter. Read on in 2 Samuel to find out his ultimate demise, a horrific end.

Finally and most incredibly, when I wrote, "Certainly He knows we will have a period of mourning things in our lives. I don't know what that period should be, for it is different for everyone. But I do know that when we think we can't go on, He gives us an alternative." How could I have known I would hear that King David would choose after three years, his time of mourning, to "be reunited with his son Absalom"?

I don't know about you, but I can't stop the tears. I wrote this all *before* He confirmed it by His Word for me, for us.

The New Testament reading for May 28 was the following:

> After saying all these things, Jesus looked up to heaven and said, "Father, the hour has come. Glorify your Son so he can give glory back to you. For you have given him authority over everyone. He gives eternal life to each one you have given him. And this is the way to have eternal life—to know you, the only true God, and Jesus Christ, the one you sent to earth. I brought glory to you here on earth by completing the work you gave me to do. Now, Father, bring me into the glory we shared before the world began. "I have revealed you to the ones you gave me from this world. They were always yours. You gave them to me, and they have kept your word. Now they know that everything I have is a gift from you, for I have passed on to them the message you gave me. They accepted it and know that I came from you, and they believe you sent me. "My prayer is not for the world, but for those you have given me, because they belong to you. All who are mine belong to you, and you have given them to me, so they bring me glory. Now

I am departing from the world; they are staying in this world, but I am coming to you. Holy Father, you have given me your name; now protect them by the power of your name so that they will be united just as we are. During my time here, I protected them by the power of the name you gave me. I guarded them so that not one was lost, except the one headed for destruction, as the Scriptures foretold. "Now I am coming to you. I told them many things while I was with them in this world so they would be filled with my joy. I have given them your word. And the world hates them because they do not belong to the world, just as I do not belong to the world. I'm not asking you to take them out of the world, but to keep them safe from the evil one. They do not belong to this world any more than I do. Make them holy by your truth; teach them your word, which is truth. Just as you sent me into the world, I am sending them into the world. And I give myself as a holy sacrifice for them so they can be made holy by your truth. "I am praying not only for these disciples but also for all who will ever believe in me through their message. I pray that they will all be one, just as you and I are one—as you are in me, Father, and I am in you. And may they be in us so that the world will believe you sent me. "I have given them the glory you gave me, so they may be one as we are one. I am in them and you are in me. May they experience such perfect unity that the world will know that you sent me and that you love them as much as you love me. Father, I want these whom you have given me to be with me where I am. Then they can see all the glory you gave me because you loved me even before the world began! "O righteous Father, the world doesn't know you, but I do; and these disciples know you sent me. I have revealed you to them, and I will continue to do so. Then your love for me will be in them, and I will be in them."

—John 17:1–26, NLT

When I wrote, "You are never alone," how could I have known Jesus would be speaking on this day and in this way to offer Himself as our hope?

As this is true, we can never, ever be alone!

This was the psalm reading for May 28:

I am worn out waiting for your rescue, but I have put my hope in your word. My eyes are straining to see your promises come true, when will you comfort me? I am shriveled like a wineskin in the smoke, but I have not forgotten to obey your decrees. How long must

I wait? When will you punish those who perse-
cute me? These arrogant people who hate your
instructions have dug deep pits to trap me.
All your commands are trustworthy. Protect
me from those who hunt me down without
cause. They almost finished me off, but I
refused to abandon your commandments. In
your unfailing love, spare my life; then I can
continue to obey your laws. Your eternal word,
O Lord, stands firm in heaven. Your faithfulness extends to every generation, as enduring as
the earth you created. Your regulations remain
true to this day, for everything serves your
plans. If your instructions hadn't sustained me
with joy, I would have died in misery. I will
never forget your commandments, for by them
you give me life. I am yours; rescue me! For I
have worked hard at obeying your commandments. Though the wicked hide along the way
to kill me, I will quietly keep my mind on your
laws. Even perfection has its limits, but your
commands have no limit.

—PSALM 119:81–96

How could I have known in offering the Romans 5:3–
5 passage in my morning writings how closely aligned it
would be with this psalm?

And finally, this all ties in with the acrostic God had
me offer:

H — He
O — Offers
P — People
E — Everything

Here is the proverb for May 28, 2009:

> Unfailing love and faithfulness make atone-
> ment for sin. By fearing the LORD, people avoid
> evil. When people's lives please the LORD, even
> their enemies are at peace with them.
>
> —PROVERBS 16:6–7, NLT

How could I have known God was going to give us a
heads-up on His "unfailing love and faithfulness"? We
call such love and faithfulness—His Son—our HOPE.

I couldn't have presented a word of this book, and most
especially this chapter, without His supernatural inter-
vention. As He has guided these words, I continue to, as
the Lewis quote offers, "give up myself to His personality." And this, my dear readers, expressed through
writing, helping others, praying for others, and serving
others, causes me, according to Lewis, "to have a real
personality of my own."

"How can I know when I am truly free in Christ?"

This is the final question posed in the Introduction. We know we are truly free in Christ when we realize Romans 5:5–6, 8:

> And this hope will not lead to disappointment. For we know how dearly God loves us, because he has given us the Holy Spirit to fill our hearts with his love. When we were utterly helpless, Christ came at just the right time and died for us sinners....But God showed his great love for us by sending Christ to die for us while we were still sinners. (NLT)

After I finalized this chapter, I met with one of my sisters in Christ, Christa. On my way to meet her, I was listening to Family Life Radio, a Christian station, in my car. They were directing listeners to a new Web site, Hope-4Heroes.org, where you can support our veterans. Hmm, haven't I been talking about freedom, veterans, and, of course, hope? This is probably just another coincidence.

When I met with Christa, she gave me a gift of a blank journal. On its cover was one word, *hope*. She hadn't a clue as to what I had been writing earlier!

Seriously, I couldn't make this stuff up! God and His coincidences—what more can I say here? Not a thing. God has said it all.

Chapter 5

IN GOLF, THE SCORE IS SETTLED; *WITH GOD,* HE SETTLES THE SCORE

ODAY IS FRIDAY, November 13, and we are nearing the end of this eleven-month journey. Today is my last planned day to commit my thoughts to you on this book. Undoubtedly there will be some final cleanup and a bit of my own editing before I send the manuscript to my publisher, but if all goes as planned I would like to have it to them around Thanksgiving.

I have much to be thankful for, indeed!

I was finishing chapter 4 when I started writing this chapter. Unfortunately, I got hung up on its title. I remembered what I had written in the Introduction about how "no golfer can predict with any specificity at the beginning of a round of golf the score to be recorded." I was trying to come up with something clever to make for a strong finish, but I was stumped. So, God had me get up out of my comfy office chair and take Pookie for a walk.

She is always ready for her walk, or even for a romp around the house, as you may recall the "Pookie incident," where God started *Ace's* journey. It is only fitting,

I suspect, that He chose to end the book having her somehow involved.

As she and I headed out onto the street, I felt especially safe, as I was equipped with my "coyote stick." It is a piece of rebar that a neighbor gave to Bob to fend off any would-be attacks. As we live in a golfing retirement community, many "coyote sticks" for other dog-walkers are 7- or 8-irons!

While Pookie sniffed every flower, rock, bush, and fire hydrant, my mind wandered to the title for this chapter. One of our neighbors came out of his home to retrieve his mail, and I thought, *I wonder if he thinks, "What in the world is she doing wearing an Arizona Cardinals' Kurt Warner youth jersey?"* If Bob had been with me, he would have said, "Honey, people aren't always thinking about you." He knows me so well. I realized I was being my typical self-involved self and not "giving my personality to Him."

And then God sent me the title: "In Golf, the Score Is Settled. With God, He Settles the Score." My first thought was, *Maybe that is too harsh*, but then I remembered Scripture, specifically this one:

> For God did not give us a spirit of timidity, but a spirit of power, of love and of self-discipline. So do not be ashamed to testify about our Lord, or ashamed of me his prisoner. But join with me in suffering for the gospel, by the

power of God, who has saved us and called us to a holy life—not because of anything we have done but because of his own purpose and grace. This grace was given us in Christ Jesus before the beginning of time, but it has now been revealed through the appearing of our Savior, Christ Jesus, who has destroyed death and has brought life and immortality to light through the gospel. And of this gospel I was appointed a herald and an apostle and a teacher. That is why I am suffering as I am. Yet I am not ashamed, because I know whom I have believed, and am convinced that he is able to guard what I have entrusted to him for that day.

—2 Timothy 1:7–12

As Pookie and I rounded the corner for home, I realized that to know true freedom in Him we must realize our journeys are not about us, but they are all about Him. It is therefore our responsibility to tell others about those journeys in whatever manner we are able.

While a golfer checks the scorecard at the end of the round for accuracy, his or her playing partner will then attest to that particular score. The score then is settled.

With God, although He loves each one of us and allows us to choose Him freely, He will settle the score with those who don't make that choice. Again, I believe, and Pastor Lee has confirmed in sermon after sermon, that God gives each of us on this earth every opportunity—even when we stand before Him in heaven, more than likely—to acknowledge, accept, and affirm Him as our Savior.

Yet clearly there will still be some who remain in the two "no" groups I wrote about in chapter 1. Remember the first "no" bunch? This is the "No, I will figure things out on my own" group. I can totally empathize with this group, as I am a "have to do things on my own or they won't be right" person, too! I still struggle with that, but I finally had to admit to myself that no matter how hard I try, things are going to happen that are out of my control and that will affect me. There is no getting around that fact. There are others who are going to impact my life, possibly in a way that I would rather not prefer. However, perhaps others will impact it in a positive way. The point is, things happen, and I can't control them all!

The second "no" group is the group that says, "No, I can't believe in a God who would allow such bad things into my life. And then you want me to praise Him? No thanks."

I made so many poor choices on my own as a youth, which culminated into a failed marriage. But when I was at the lowest point in my life, God sent me Bob. I know without a doubt, had I not made the sorrowful choices of my youth, I would not now know the joy life holds when you choose Jesus. Please don't misunderstand; I am not advocating my readers to make bad choices to know good ones! The point is, I was blind then but now I see.

Maybe you are in a situation where you claim, "Carolyn, my whole life has been a low point." I ask you to search your heart for just one good thing in your life. If you can't come up with one thing or person or event, I want to pray for you. I want you to go to my Web site, www.heartofthecrossbooks.com. Use the Contact feature and send me your prayer need. By the time *Ace* is published there may be a Prayer tab on the site. I haven't figured it out yet, but God will.

I honestly do not want you to go through your life thinking you don't have one good thing to come from God. You now have someone who will pray for you, and that could have only come from God. I realize I may be opening myself up for a flood of requests, but if it means you might draw closer to God because you know just one person cares, then so be it. Bring it on!

My sin was nailed on the cross with Jesus. So was yours. If you think you don't have any sin for which you need forgiveness, I encourage you to search your heart and reconsider. We all sin. There is no getting around it. Maybe you told a little white lie. Maybe you were critical to or about someone else. Maybe you felt hatred for another. Maybe you took our Lord's name in vain. Maybe, maybe...you fill in the blanks.

> ... There is no one righteous, not even one.
>
> —ROMANS 3:10

If His death weren't enough, as well it should be, there is another undeniable blessing we Christians have, to be sure, and that is God's message of hope in His Son's return.

> All this is evidence that God's judgment is right, and as a result you will be counted worthy of the kingdom of God, for which you are suffering. God is just: He will pay back trouble to those who trouble you and give relief to you who are troubled, and to us as well. This will happen when the Lord Jesus is revealed from heaven in blazing fire with his powerful angels. He will punish those who do not know God and do not obey the gospel of our Lord Jesus. They will be punished with everlasting destruction and shut out from the presence of the Lord and from the majesty of his power on the day he comes to be glorified in his holy people and to be marveled at among all those who have believed. This includes you because you believed our testimony to you.
>
> —2 THESSALONIANS 1:5–10

As I said earlier, I hesitated to be so bold in my closing

remarks but felt compelled to do so. God does not want one of us to be punished or shut out from Him. But clearly the choice is ours.

At the end of the age, God will settle the score.

> Be careful that you do not refuse to listen to the One who is speaking. For if the people of Israel did not escape when they refused to listen to Moses, the earthly messenger, we will certainly not escape if we reject the One who speaks to us from heaven!
>
> —HEBREWS 12:25, NLT

So, if God's own Word, along with my golf metaphors of keeping things simple, course management, and staying hopeful, are still not enough to keep you or someone you love out of a "no" group, let's look logically at the benefits of making a choice for Him.

Our Creator could have easily forced us all to feel freedom in Him, couldn't He? Instead, He gave each of us the capacity to choose Him or not.

As Bob and I read Scripture on June 2, 2009, he commented, "Gee, those boys of the Old Testament were sure fickle characters. One minute they are for Moses, the next minute not. Then later they are for David, then Absalom, then David again, and then Sheba. What is up with that?"

Yes, it is true; we can all be fickle choosing what we

want, what may be popular, or what may be based on our needs at the time.

It seems to me a "choice" for God is made up of three components.

- Choosing to *acknowledge* God
- Choosing to *align* with God
- Choosing to *affirm* God

Before you or someone else can move toward a choice in Him, let's look at a couple of questions.

- Do you believe your existence in this world is for yourself alone? Yes or No.
- (If you answered yes, then proceed to the next question.)

- If existing for yourself is the reason you are here, why would God give you the opportunity to choose to acknowledge Him or not?

- Does it make sense that the answer to the second question is, "He wouldn't; you wouldn't have a choice"?

- Is it reasonable to believe that we are then here for one reason alone—to choose Him or not?

- (If you believe there is any reason other than that, please feel free to write it below.)

- If, however, you can comfortably agree with me that we are here to choose Him or not, let's go a bit further. If you choose not to, I will pray your heart to be open and that you will go on reading.

- If you can choose to acknowledge Him, then shouldn't you choose to align with Him and His Word?

Hopefully that makes sense. If you agree, let's take the next step.

- If you acknowledge Him and align with His Word, then shouldn't you choose to affirm His plans for your life? The word *affirm* is from the Latin *affimire,* "to make firm." As a verb, *to affirm* is used to "express dedication to."[5]

Ah...that may be a sticky point. Here is where the notion of freedom comes into play. Here is where you have to choose to believe God to be your Pilot and that you are the passenger—*or not.*

- So can you affirm God's plans for your life,
  even if those plans do not always have a
  positive outcome? Meaning, can you offer
  Him praise through the storms of your
  life?

If you answered yes, then you understand freedom in God.

Do you recall I wrote the following about tragedy in chapter 1: "With any tragedy, the obvious question is, why does God allow such things to occur? I don't presume to know why God allows things to happen as they do. All I can offer is, perhaps He places before each of us circumstances in which we have the choice to willingly serve Him in whatever way we can, whatever those circumstances happen to be."

Do you recall in chapter 2, I used the same explanation for the good times?

Both sets of circumstances involve our choice. It must be this way if we are to be truly free in Him!

So how can we know when we are truly free in Christ? Let's go back to *Ace's* beginning:

> The more we let God take us over, the more
> truly ourselves we become—because he made
> us. He invented all the different people that
> you and I were intended to be. It is when I
> turn to Christ, when I give up myself to His

personality, that I first begin to have a real personality of my own.

—C. S. Lewis[6]

Here's something from me based on this journey:

When I choose to simply acknowledge, align with, and affirm God, He and I have a freeing relationship based in Jesus Christ.

If you have reached this point in the book and you are in the "yes" group already or have jumped on over from one of the "no" groups, then you are smack dab in the middle of an A.C.E.:

A — A
C — Celebration of His
E — Everlasting freedom extended to everyone

Party on! You don't have to try to find that swing to raise your anticipation and expectation of scoring an ace; you have found it and can continue your journey with God!

To my golfing readers, I must now apologize for switching to a football metaphor, but at this point in the story, I feel as if it is fourth and goal with one second left in the game. I want you or that someone you love to get into the end zone! Please don't get "blitzed" by complicated thoughts, a sorrowful heart, or hopelessness in your life! You have already been invited to God's Super Bowl. You have your own invitation, and your seat is in the luxurious owner's box!

To: Everyone on Earth

From: God, Christ, and the Holy Spirit

You are cordially invited to join us in celebrating each day of your life

RSVP: Anytime, any day

No presents necessary. We will supply the grace.

Just bring yourselves and your open heart. You may also want to bring along a tissue, for some of our celebrations may bring on tears.

Hope to see you soon!

As I conclude, it is mid-November 2009, the height of football season. I can recall as if it were yesterday seeing Kurt Warner, the now retired quarterback for the Cardinals, on television grinning ear to ear after winning the 2008–2009 NFC championship game. The team was headed to the Super Bowl, and it appeared as if confetti was raining from the sky. Warner was thanking Jesus Christ profusely for all He had done in his life and for taking them on that journey. Unfortunately, the Cardinals didn't win, but Warner became a Christian fan favorite that day.

After Pookie and I came into the house from our walk, I looked down on my jersey and realized I was wearing number thirteen. Here I am writing to you on Friday the thirteenth wearing number thirteen, a number belonging to one of God's own. I had no idea when I got dressed this morning about the coincidence, but God did. Whoa!

C'mon, let's celebrate; let's live each day as if it were our last and thank our God, our One and only ACE!

EPILOGUE

I N CLOSING *Ace: One in Golf and One with God*, I was focused on football. Like other sports, football has strategy, offense, and defense. Each week, players and coaches alike prepare for battle. It occurs to me that as a golfer approaches the game, he or she has weapons for battle too. It seems fitting to prepare to discuss that weaponry as I gear up for a new book in the G.O.L.F. series, *Fore: Spiritual Weapons for Christians*. For my non-golfing readers, *fore* means "watch out."

Until then, "Peace to the brothers, and love with faith from God the Father and the Lord Jesus Christ. Grace to all who love our Lord Jesus Christ with an undying love" (Ephesians 6:23–24). I know you may not believe me, but I randomly opened the Bible to see what God wanted me to finish with for you, and He offered this verse from Ephesians.

And what scripture do you suppose was in bold lettering in my Bible just before the verse above? Coincidentally, it fits with the topic of *Fore: Spiritual Weapons for Christians*.

> Put on the full armor of God so that you can take your stand against the devil's schemes.
>
> —Ephesians 6:11

To Contact the Author

WWW.HEARTOFTHECROSSBOOKS.COM

First book in the G.O.L.F. Series

MULLIGAN:

A Second Chance at True Love and God's Grace

In golf, there's a term for a second chance— a mulligan—in which a golfer has the opportunity to retake an errant shot.

What do you wish you could do over?

After a failed first marriage, Carolyn Snelling knew that God had given her the best in the form of her second husband, Bob. In fact, he provided her with an example of Christ's unconditional love, which led her to a saving relationship with Jesus Christ. Through her new life in the Lord and her remarriage, Snelling has learned that the God she serves truly is a God of second chances.

ISBN-13: 978-1-59979-528-7

Second book in the G.O.L.F. Series

Eagle:

Two Under Par and Soaring for God

**In golf, an eagle translates
into being two under par
on any given golf hole.
Being under par is a mark
of excellence in golf.**

Are you ready to soar like an eagle for Christ?

The second feature in the G.O.L.F. series, Eagle once
again uses golf references to underscore key principles
that are sure to help you reach new heights in your relationship with God. In her unique, conversational style,
Snelling shares personal anecdotes and tales of her own
struggles as she explains the importance of maintaining
a well-balanced life and focusing every day on Christ.

ISBN-13: 978-1-59979-851-6

NOTES

1.   C. S. Lewis quote accessed at Rick Warren, "Worship, The Barrier of Pride," *Purpose-Driven Connection: Daily Hope*, http://profile.purposedriven.com/dailyhope/post. html?contentid=3395, January 13, 2010.

2.   Ibid.

3.   Ibid.

4.   "History," The Daughters of the Republic of Texas, The Alamo Web site, www.thealamo.org, January 14, 2010. For this and more information about the Alamo, visit www.thealamo. org/history.html.

5.   Definition of *affirm* available at www.merriam-webster. com (accessed January 22, 2010).

6.   C. S. Lewis quote, from Rick Warren, *Purpose-Driven Connection: Daily Hope*.

Upcoming Releases...

Fore: Spiritual Weapons for Christians

Groove: In Golf and with God